PRELUDE
Op. 28, No. 7

PIN
Arr. by Leon Block

Slowly

PRELUDE
Op. 28, No. 20

FRÉDÉRIC CHOPIN
Arr. by Leon Block

Largo

WALTZ
Op.18

FRÉDÉRIC CHOPIN
Arr. by Leon Block

WALTZ
Op. 34 No. 2

FRÉDÉRIC CHOPIN
Arr. by Leon Block

D.C. al Fine

WALTZ
Op. 64, No.2

FRÉDÉRIC CHOPIN
Arr. by Leon Block

Moderato

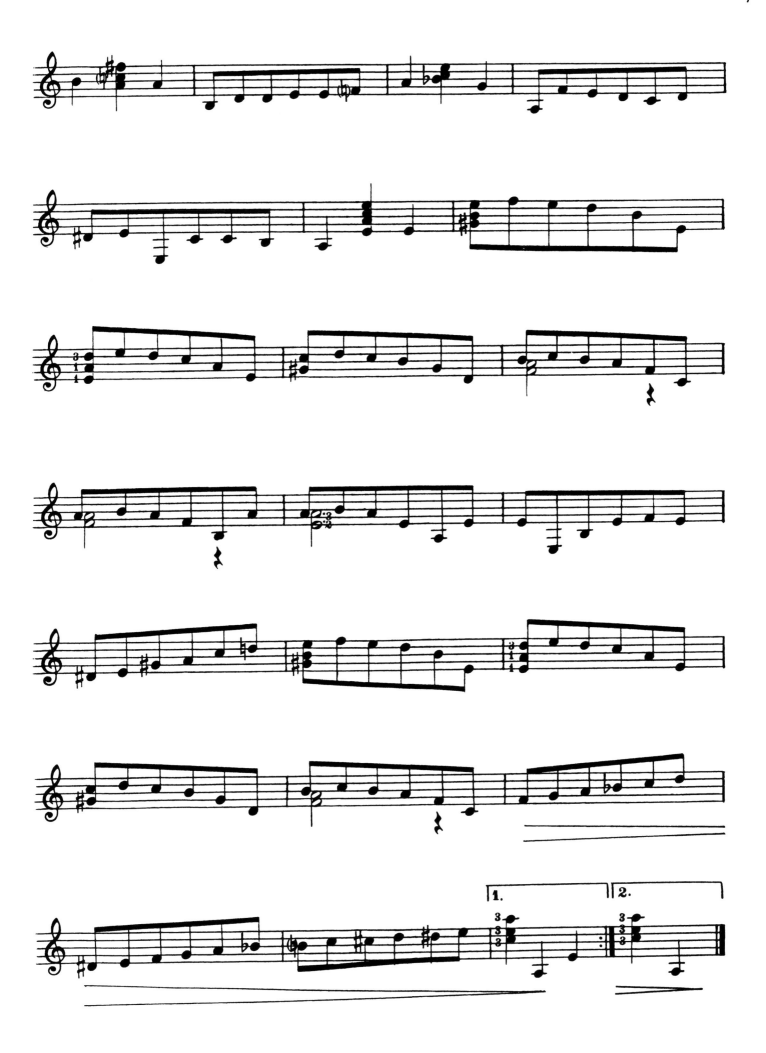

WALTZ
(Posthumous)

FRÉDÉRIC CHOPIN
Arr. by Leon Block

(Arpeggio)

D.C. al Fine

NOCTURNE
Op. 9, No. 2

FRÉDÉRIC CHOPIN
Arr. by Leon Block

FUNERAL MARCH

FRÉDÉRIC CHOPIN
Arr. by Leon Block

Andante

p

Fine

D. C. al Fine

MAZURKA
Op.68, No. 2

FRÉDÉRIC CHOPIN
Arr. by Leon Block

MAZURKA
Op.7, No.2

FRÉDÉRIC CHOPIN
Arr. by Leon Block

Moderately fast

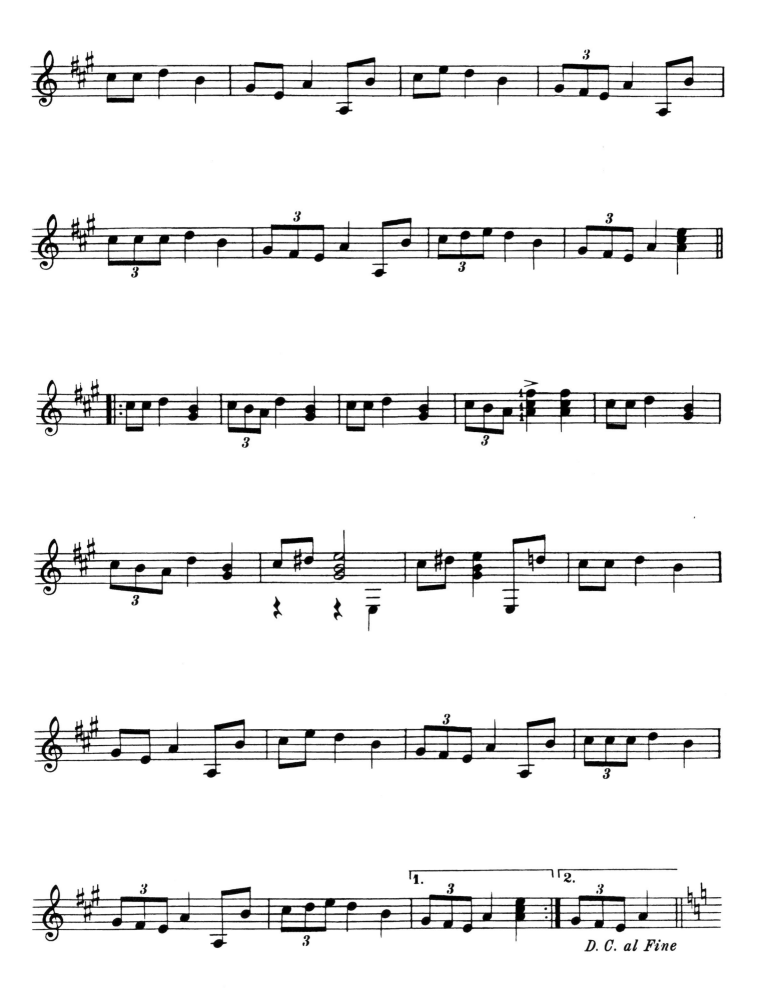

D. C. al Fine

MAZURKA
Op. 7, No. 1

FRÉDÉRIC CHOPIN
Arr. by Leon Block

D. C. al Fine